ASSURANCE
for a
LIFETIME

ASSURANCE

for a

LIFETIME

MARILYN MEBERG

THOMAS NELSON
Since 1798

NASHVILLE   DALLAS   MEXICO CITY   RIO DE JANEIRO   BEIJING

Assurance for a Lifetime

Published in Nashville, Tennessee. Thomas Nelson is a trademark of Thomas Nelson, Inc.

Thomas Nelson, Inc. titles may be purchased in bulk for educational, business, fundraising, or sales promotional use. For information, please email SpecialMarkets@ThomasNelson.com.

Unless otherwise indicated, Scripture quotations used in this book are from The Holy Bible, New Living Translation (NLT), copyright © 1996 by Tyndale House Publishers, Inc., Wheaton, IL 60189. Used by permission.

Other Scripture references are from the following sources:

The Holy Bible, New International Version (NIV). Copyright © 1973, 1978, 1984, International Bible Society. Used by permission of Zondervan Bible Publishers.

The Message (MSG), copyright © 2002. Used by permission of NavPress Publishing Group.

The New King James Version (NKJV®), copyright 1979, 1980, 1982, Thomas Nelson, Inc., Publishers.

Library of Congress Cataloging-in-Publication Data

Meberg, Marilyn.
    The assurance for a lifetime / by Marilyn Meberg.
      p. cm.
    ISBN-10: 0-8499-4500-3
    ISBN-13: 978-0-8499-4500-7
    1. Christian life. I. Title.
BV4501.3.M435 2004
248.4—dc22   2004000519

Printed in the United States of America

08 09 10 11 OPM 10 9 8 7

CONTENTS

INTRODUCTION:
YOU ARE A CHRISTIAN

Here's a conversation I've never had: "Marilyn, I'm struggling with knowing if I am a Democrat or a Republican."

"Sounds serious. Are you registered in either party?"

"Oh yes. I'm a registered Republican, but every now and then I think I might be a closet Democrat. I lose sleep over this."

"Well, let's review your voting record. Did you vote for Senator Givitaway or Dr. Hangontwit?"

"Well, actually I voted for Senator Whatever, but I think he slides in and out of both parties."

Though that conversation never occurred, here's one I've had repeatedly.

"Marilyn, I don't really think I'm a Christian. I lose sleep over this."

"Well, let's look at your history. Have you come to Jesus, confessed your sin, received His forgiveness, and asked Him to come into your heart and life where He promises to stay with you forever?"

"Oh yes. I've done that a bunch of times."

"Well, since you can't become a bunch of Christians, you don't need to ask a bunch of times."

"But I still have doubts about whether I did it right—or if it even happened. It seemed too simple. Actually I think it would be a lot easier if all I had to worry about is whether I'm a Republican or a Democrat."

The reality is, you don't need to worry about any of those issues (unless you're really committed to Senator Whatever). God wants you to feel assured that you absolutely became a Christian the minute you prayed your prayer receiving Christ into your heart and life. That divine transaction may seem simple, but it is profoundly life changing.

Let's take a minute and run through the steps

you took to know God personally through the life, death, and resurrection of Jesus Christ.

1. You recognized your sin condition. First John 1:8 says, "If we claim to be without sin, we deceive ourselves and the truth is not in us" (NIV).

2. You confessed your sin. First John 1:9 says, "But if we confess our sins to him, he is faithful and just to forgive us and to cleanse us from every wrong."

3. You realized Jesus is the only way for you to have a relationship with God. In John 14:6, Jesus said, "I am the way, the truth, and the life. No one can come to the Father except through me."

4. You believed and received Jesus as your Savior. John 1:12 assures us, "But to all who believed him and accepted him, he gave the right to become children of God."

Now we're reviewing this list together, and you're nodding your head and mumbling, "Yeah, yeah, I did that. OK, yeah, I did that." But maybe one thing that is hanging you up is this: You may *believe*, but you aren't sure you've *received*. There is an important difference between the two actions. I can believe something and not do a thing about it. (For example, I can believe I have broccoli stuck in my front teeth and in spite of the evidence of its presence and my profound belief in its existence, if I do nothing about it, believing doesn't change anything. I am still sporting broccoli in my teeth.) We need to act on what we believe.

One of the most compelling invitations to action is stated in Revelation 3:20:

"Look! Here I stand at the door and knock. If you hear me calling and open the door, I will come in." The picture is of Jesus seeking entrance into our lives by knocking on the heart's door, making Himself known and waiting upon our response. Acting upon our belief means opening the door and asking Him to come in. He then comes in and inhabits our life forever. He also walks through life with us forever.

If you think you have believed but have not acted upon that belief, let me encourage you to act this very minute. You could pray this simple prayer:

Lord Jesus, I believe in You. I've confessed my sin. But now I want to act upon my belief. I am opening the door of my heart and life to You. Please come in. Stay with me forever! Thank You that You will. Thank You for loving me. Amen.

King David, in Psalm 118:21, said to God, "I thank you for answering my prayer and saving me!" You can say the same thing. God heard your prayer. He saved you. You can stop worrying and losing sleep. You *are* a Christian.

The purpose of this little booklet is not only to increase your assurance that you are a Christian but also to answer the question, "What do I do now?"

You may be glad to know there is nothing you have to do. There is instead some great learning to be done. This booklet is meant to encourage and educate you about your decision of a lifetime. I promise it won't be boring. I can't stand to be bored, so if nothing else, this has to keep me from slipping into a coma as well as you. Grab a cup of something, and let's settle in for a little visit. It will be a good time.

WANDERING IN LIFE'S PARKING LOT, LOOKING FOR FORGIVENESS

I loved the newspaper account of a feisty elderly lady who, having completed her grocery shopping, headed for her car only to see four guys in the act of driving off with it. She dropped her shopping bags, yanked a handgun from her purse, and yelled, "I have a gun, and I know how to use it! Get out of that car!" The four men leaped out and ran for cover.

With shaky hands, the lady then loaded her groceries in the backseat, slid behind the wheel, and attempted to put the key in the ignition. After several unsuccessful attempts, it dawned on her it wasn't just her nerves that prevented the key from fitting. She was in the wrong car. Hers was parked four spaces away.

With great chagrin, she threw the groceries into her own car and took off for the police station. Apologetically she told her story to the police sergeant, who fell into a pile laughing. Unable to regain his composure, he simply pointed to four pale and shaken men at the end of the counter. They had just reported a hijacking by an elderly lady toting a gun. No charges were filed.

Our little gun-toting grandma didn't have a firm grasp on some crucial facts. She knew she had a car, and she knew the general vicinity of where she'd parked it. But she lost sight of the specific spot.

I wonder if many of you might have something in common with the gun-toter. You probably will skip the gun, but maybe you're wandering in life's parking lot confused about some major questions having to do with God's forgiveness. Those questions keep you several spaces away from where you need to be. Questions like, "Aren't there some sins that are too disgusting even for God to forgive? Isn't it reasonable that He has to draw the line somewhere—and maybe I've crossed that line?

Isn't there also something in the Bible about an unforgivable sin?"

The Bible has answers for those unsettling questions. Many verses assure you that your sins are forgiven, but take a look at these four in particular:

Psalm 103:3: "He forgives all my sins."

Romans 4:7–8: "Oh, what joy for those whose disobedience is forgiven, whose sins are put out of sight. Yes, what joy for those whose sin is no longer counted against them by the Lord."

Acts 10:43: "Everyone who believes in him will have their sins forgiven through his name."

Psalm 103:12: "He has removed our rebellious acts as far away from us as the east is from the west."

Do you see anything that would imply that God will forgive some sins but not others? Do you find any words that suggest there are conditions for God's forgiveness?

Since most people probably put conditions on their forgiveness of you, and certainly many of them have a line you'd better not cross, it's understandable that you would assume God operates in the same way. The fact that He *doesn't* operate that way throws us. We're not used to experiencing "it's forgiven and forgotten." Because it is so foreign to our experience, we question it. But you'd have to rewrite the Bible to support the idea that God has a limit on what He will forgive. The Bible says He forgives *all* confessed sin. Period!

"But wait a minute," you say. "What about the unforgivable sin I've read about? If it's unforgivable, that means there is a limit to what God forgives. What is the unforgivable sin, and how can I know I haven't committed it?"

The Bible does mention an unforgivable sin. We should discuss that fact so you can have absolute assurance that you haven't committed it.

There is only one passage in Scripture that refers to an unforgivable sin. It's Matthew 12:31–32, which describes a time when Jesus was totally exasperated with the Pharisees, a religious group trailing Jesus around. They were hoping to catch Him in some wrongdoing so they could further criticize Him and convince people He was dangerous, a fraud, and a social rabble-rouser who should be killed. They claimed the miracles Jesus was performing came from the power of Satan, and they refused to believe Jesus's work was that of the Holy Spirit of God working in and through Jesus. The Pharisees couldn't deny the fact that what Jesus was doing was obviously supernatural. So, instead of acknowledging the truth and giving credit to God, they said His power was satanic. For Jesus, it would appear that accusation was the last straw. He cut loose with, "Every sin or blasphemy can be forgiven—except blasphemy against the Holy Spirit, which can never be forgiven."

So what does that mean for you? Is there any way it could apply to your sin? Remember, Scripture says, "Everyone who believes in him will have their sins forgiven through his name" (Acts 10:43). No matter how bad your sins, there is forgiveness for them. So, in essence, we have to say there is no unforgivable *sin*, but there is an unforgivable *condition*. That is the condition of unbelief. There is no forgiveness for the one who refuses to believe. There is no forgiveness for the one who dies and never asks for forgiveness. There are people who couldn't care less about sin and what it does to the body and soul. They couldn't care less what that means for eternity. Those who never seek forgiveness are committing the unforgivable sin. They have chosen that condition for themselves. God would forgive them if they asked. But if they don't, they experience the eternal consequence.

So I ask you: Can you, by any stretch of the imagination, think you've committed the unforgivable sin? Not a chance! If you had, you wouldn't care enough about your spiritual life to even wonder about that sin. You wouldn't be reading this booklet. You simply would not be interested in any spiritual issues. Why? Because you would be living in total unbelief.

Perhaps now the whole forgiveness issue is starting to make sense. I hope you are beginning to feel assured that you truly are a forgiven Christian. If so, you are heading for the right parking space.

There is, however, another important fact you will need to key into before there's a fit in the ignition. Let's approach that fact with a question: Is it your perception that even though God forgives sin there still is earthly punishment for that sin? Have you wondered if all the chaos in your life might be God's punishment for wrongdoing? Perhaps there's more assurance to be learned before you start your engine. We'll talk about that in the next chapter. But first, here are some questions to help you consider what we'll be discussing in these pages. The questions are intended to make you think about the steps you've taken to insure your future. If this booklet was about protecting your home or car or medical needs, we might think of them as "insurance questions." But they're much more important than that. They're designed to help you accept the fact that the commitment you've made will benefit you for all eternity. So instead let's call them . . .

Assurance Questions

1. In spite of the Scripture verses on forgiveness, do you struggle with a particular sin you committed that you still can't believe is forgiven? What is that sin?

2. Even though you realize it's not the unpardonable sin, why does it seem unpardonable to you?

3. Do you think that sin should keep you in a state of constant insecurity? Do you feel you deserve that insecurity? Is there a chance you think you should punish yourself since God isn't going to?

4. Write God a letter and tell Him everything you feel and think about that sin. Don't leave any thought or emotion out of the letter. Read it out loud to Him. Ask His forgiveness again, even though you already have. Thank Him for the fact that your sin is forgiven and does not need to be brought up again. Now go outside and bury the letter. It's now dead and buried. Leave it there.

You Aren't Being Punished

A young woman named Holly lives in emotional and circumstantial chaos. Though she is a Christian and believes God forgave her sin, she still feels she is being punished. Here's her story.

Holly found herself pregnant at the age of nineteen. Though she and the baby's father did not really love each other, they married. Holly hoped her friends and family were numerically challenged and wouldn't notice the "early" birth of their baby.

The husband was indifferent to Holly and the baby. Since he had no inclination to support the family, Holly got a job. The marriage broke up within a year.

Several years later Holly met and married a

"nice Christian man." He loved her little girl, provided financial security for the family, was active in church—and bored Holly to death.

At work, she met a man and began a seemingly innocent friendship, which ultimately became an affair and resulted in another pregnancy. Holly's husband filed for divorce. The affair ended as soon as the lover learned of the pregnancy. Holly's little girl wanted to live with her stepfather "'cause he was really nice."

Holly clearly had made some enormous mistakes, with costly human consequences. She had been raised in a Christian home. When she prayed to receive Christ into her life at the age of twelve, she was sincere. But in spite of knowing better, Holly had made some major messes. Could God forgive all she'd done? Did He love her in spite of her behavior?

She knew Scripture teaches forgiveness to those who confess their sins. Although Holly confessed and asked forgiveness, she still felt she deserved punishment. In fact, there was no doubt in her mind that she *was* being punished. How else could she interpret everything going so wrong in her life?

Here's where Holly's facts don't key into the ignition: She is right when she recognizes the Bible teaches that God forgives all sin. But she's wrong about what He does once the sin is forgiven. Here's what God says He does about forgiven sin:

"I will never again remember their sins and lawless deeds" (Hebrews 10:17).

"I, even I, am he who blots out your transgressions, for my own sake, and remembers your sins no more" (Isaiah 43:25 NIV).

How utterly mind-boggling! God forgives the sins and then puts them out of His mind. And if it's out of His mind, He's not thinking up ways to dole out punishment. He's not thinking about the sin at all! Therefore He's not punishing at all.

"But," you say, "if God is not punishing me, why does it look and feel like punishment?" It looks and feels like punishment because we confuse *consequences* with *punishment*. God does not cause the consequences. Our behavior does. God is often blamed for what we set in motion when we sin. God is not responsible for our decision to sin. Neither is He responsible for the consequences of our sin.

For example, each time Holly became pregnant, she set in motion a string of consequences. Though the first divorce relieved Holly of an uninvolved husband, he *is* the child's father. Indifferent though he may be, that little girl wants and needs a daddy who cares about her. Since that's a role the dad chooses not to play, his rejection produces security and trust issues that deeply imprint her little psyche.

Adultery in the second marriage set up difficult consequences yet again for Holly when she yielded to an immoral relationship. She once again produced a child who would experience a lack of the father's involvement. In addition to those consequences, Holly is now a single mother with limited job skills and two children to raise. Those consequences are not God's doing; they are Holly's.

Some people may assume that once God's forgiveness occurs, the consequences of their past behavior will disappear. If Holly were thinking that way, she might think God would reward her confession by inspiring her Christian husband to forgive her, accept the new baby, and provide financial well-being for all of them. That would be a great scenario, but it's an unlikely one.

These facts could all be depressing if we did not bear in mind not only that sin is forgiven but also that we don't have to repeat the sin. We can choose to avoid the pattern that sets up yet another string of consequences. Since we have a choice, we can choose wise behavior.

For example, Holly can examine her life, recognize what patterns she is prone to fall into, and then choose to live differently and avoid the destructive patterns. She can choose to commit herself to the two little lives she brought into the world. She can choose to curb her appetites and become a responsible and nurturing mother who will provide security for their emotional and physical environment.

She can also choose to honor the Spirit of God, who lives within her. When she does so, He will lead her in the direction of becoming a forgiven survivor of previous choices and not a victim. Perhaps He'll also remind her of the words of Psalm 130:3–4:

"LORD, if you kept a record of our sins, who, O Lord, could ever survive? But you offer forgiveness, that we might learn to fear you."

If you can key into that gigantic fact, you're ready to start your engine.

ASSURANCE QUESTIONS

1. Can you think of an event in your life that punished you with consequences?

2. Was that event your fault? If not, whose fault was it? What part was your responsibility?

3. Is there anything you can do now that will stop the feeling of punishment?

4. Do you feel you deserve to be punished? Is it reasonable to believe God is not punishing you but perhaps you are punishing yourself? If so, how could you change your thinking?

3

THE HOLY SPIRIT:
YOUR PERSONAL POWER PACK

You have the assurance now that you're a Christian and that your sins did not cause God to fall off His throne when you confessed them to Him. He forgave all of them and isn't punishing you for any of them. The *consequences* may be punishing, but God isn't. You're in a good place with Him, so now what?

The next step is to realize the Holy Spirit lives in you. The moment you said yes to Jesus, the Holy Spirit entered your interior world, which motivates and guides your exterior world. The Holy Spirit literally lives in you and, in so doing, wants to teach you new ways of living.

Many people have misconceptions about who

the Holy Spirit is and how He operates. For example, our son, Jeff, informed us at age seven that he didn't feel comfortable with "Christian stuff." When I tried to probe his little heart and mind, he finally admitted he was nervous about the "Holy Ghost." He thought it was spooky to have a ghost inside him. Jeff didn't think it was necessary for the ghost to be there in the first place, and he had no idea how to "keep tabs" on it because the ghost was invisible.

Jeff's aversion to "Christian stuff" made perfect sense to me then. In some very early translations of the Bible, the phrase *Holy Ghost* is used instead of *Holy Spirit*. The two phrases mean the same. Apparently Jeff's Sunday school teacher preferred the term *Holy Ghost*. Surely if she'd thought about it, she would have known that image would put her little students on edge, but she was either indifferent to their concerns or ignorant of them. Whatever her mind-set, she and I had a chat about her wording. The result was that the ghost disappeared.

When Jeff was in junior high school and fully

recovered from the "ghost thing," he began to refer to the Holy Spirit as the "Force." Jeff loved the *Star Wars* series and felt the Holy Spirit and George Lucas's "Force" had a lot in common. We had another clarifying talk about the Holy Spirit as I pointed out the Holy Spirit is not some impersonal power that does magic tricks. (I'm happy to report that Jeff is going to be forty his next birthday and appears to have settled his misconceptions about the Holy Spirit.)

Possibly you, too, have misconceptions about the Holy Spirit. Who is He, how does He operate, and what does it mean to have Him living within you?

The answer to the question of who He is, is simple: He is God. However, while the answer is simple, understanding it is not so simple. The Holy Spirit is the third part of the Trinity. The Trinity is composed of three divine entities: God the Father, Jesus the Son, and the Holy Spirit. All those entities have separate roles, but *all* are God. (Try explaining *that* to a kid who's already leery about an inhabiting ghost!)

We must recognize that much of God is a mystery and often beyond our comprehension. The Trinity is one of those mysteries.

The most unsatisfactory Trinity explanation I heard as a child was that the Trinity could be likened to an egg. The egg is made up of three parts—the yolk, the white, and the shell—but it still is one thing: an egg. Since I liked the yolk and not the white and certainly the shell wasn't appealing, I wondered what part of the Trinity I was rejecting. I hoped it wasn't Jesus because He was the one who forgave my sins. The other two Trinity parts weren't clear to me, so I tried not to think about them.

But here's what is clear: The Holy Spirit of God is your personal power pack. As you continue your Christian walk, it's fantastic to know that living within you is this Spirit who means to give you the power to begin new ways of living.

We'll get back to that fact in subsequent chapters, but first let's do a quick trace on the Holy Spirit's power as it is written about in the Old and New Testaments.

The Holy Spirit appears at the beginning of creation: "The earth was empty, a formless mass cloaked in darkness. And the Spirit of God was hovering over its surface" (Genesis 1:2). Don't you love that image? From that hovering presence came all creation! As Psalm 33:8–9 states, "Let everyone in the world fear the LORD, and let everyone stand in awe of him. For when he spoke, the world began! It appeared at his command."

The Holy Spirit not only spoke the world into being, but that same awesome power is made available to people—to you and me! We read of repeated instances in the Old Testament where the Holy Spirit came upon various persons who received strength to do something they had no prior strength to do. For example, a young man named Samson experienced an unexpected Holy Spirit moment. You can read Samson's full story in the book of Judges. It is fascinating.

"As Samson and his parents were going down to Timnah, a young lion attacked Samson near the vineyards of Timnah. At that moment the

Spirit of the LORD powerfully took control of him, and he ripped the lion's jaws apart with his bare hands" (Judges 14:5–6). Make a mental note to remember this passage. Later we're going to apply it to *you*.

Also in the Old Testament, we read about King David's leadership skills that were made possible because of the Holy Spirit. David was an uneducated shepherd. How could he become the king of Israel? How did he know what to do and how to do it? Read 1 Samuel 16:13 to find out.

Now let's turn our attention to a few New Testament accounts of the Holy Spirit. One of the most mind-stretching accounts of Holy Spirit power concerns the Virgin Mary. Here's the story as told in Luke 1:34–35:

"Mary asked the angel, 'But how can I have a baby? I am a virgin.' The angel replied, 'The Holy Spirit will come upon you, and the power of the Most High will overshadow you. So the baby born to you will be holy, and he will be called the Son of God.'"

During Jesus's earthly ministry, the Spirit descended on Him like a dove as He was baptized by John the Baptist (see Mark 1:10). Luke 4:1, 14 describes how Jesus was filled with and guided by the Spirit. And in the power of that Spirit, Jesus cast out demons (see Matthew 12:28).

If your eyes haven't glazed over from all these Bible references, hang in there for one more crucial Holy Spirit fact: Jesus told the disciples that after He died and was resurrected, He would send the "Spirit of truth," who would teach His followers everything they would need to know about communicating Jesus to the world (see John 15:26; Acts 1:8). That Spirit-filled truth telling gave birth to the first-century church.

Now here we are in the twenty-first century, and other Spirit-powered persons have communicated Jesus to *you*. You heard, believed, and received. The day you said yes to Him, the Holy Spirit gave you a new birth and a new life. Jesus called that experience being born again.

There's a perfect description of the new you in Titus 3:5–6:

"He saved us, not because of the good things we did, but because of his mercy. He washed away our sins and gave us a new life through the Holy Spirit. He generously poured out the Spirit upon us because of what Jesus Christ our Savior did."

Just as the Holy Spirit hovered over the earth that was once "cloaked in darkness," He also hovered over your soul and brought you from darkness to light and then into a personal relationship. You are an enlightened new you, and your new you has got the power!

ASSURANCE QUESTIONS

1. Now that you know more about the Holy Spirit, can you see that you've had some misconceptions about Him? If so, what were they?

2. What is one area of your life in which you especially need Holy Spirit power?

3. How would you explain who the Holy Spirit is to someone who does not know?

4. How would you describe how you feel about Him based on what you've learned so far?

5. Have you ever had a Holy Spirit experience? How would you describe it?

USE YOUR WHEELS!

A man named Clarence had been sitting at the bar of the Happy Hour Hotel for several hours. He'd been celebrating with some of his coworkers a completed business deal.

With horror he looked at the clock on the wall; it read 1 a.m. Knowing he'd stayed longer than he intended and that his wife would be concerned about him, he slid off the stool with the intention of quickly leaving for home. To his utter surprise, when his feet hit the floor his legs didn't support him, and he fell flat. Embarrassed, he made another attempt only to fall flat again.

Confident he'd not consumed enough to put him in such a condition, he was puzzled. Grateful that no one seemed to notice, he crawled on his hands and knees to the door, maneuvered his way out, and attempted again to stand. Again he fell.

"Well," he said, "not to worry. I only live two blocks away. I'll crawl home."

When he reached his house, he crawled through the front door and on up the stairs. Fortunately Bernadette, his wife of many years, was snoring softly and unaware of Clarence awkwardly hauling himself into bed.

The next morning Clarence awakened with Bernadette standing by the bed with a cup of hot coffee. "Well, sweetie, I guess you had a late night at the Happy Hour Hotel."

"Oh, baby," he said sheepishly, "how did you know I was there?"

"The owner called this morning and said you left without your wheelchair."

Why did Clarence forget his wheelchair? He was in a hurry and forgot he had one. In fact, he forgot he even needed one! He proved he could manage without it; after all, he did get home. But he could have gotten home more easily and quickly with his wheels; they ensured successful maneuvering.

Yes, Clarence had ready access to his wheelchair, which provided strength and help beyond what he could provide for himself. It allowed him to get from one place to another with ease. But he forgot he had it.

I have been a Christian for more than fifty years. You might think I would always remember that the power source for my life rests not in my own efforts but in the enablement of the Holy Spirit who lives within me. But there are times when, like Clarence, I forget how much I need wheels. I, too, step out on my own, and to my amazement, I fall flat.

The Holy Spirit wants to be the enablement for maneuvering me through life. I could crawl about in my own power, but why should I when there's a far better way?

Here's an example: I am an impatient woman. I want the slow driver to get out of the fast lane, the grocery-store checkout person to not chat incessantly with the woman in front of me, and for the waitress to remember I ordered iced tea and not Coke. My impatience can cause me to have abrupt responses, which I'm not proud of.

So how does remembering my inner power source help me with those mundane irritants? Quite simply, I pray to God and admit my unattractive impatience (no news to Him). As a result, I have often felt a "not-me" softening in my heart as I'm forced to slow down. Believe me, this is not something that would happen were I to attempt it on my own! Other times I've been prompted to take note of my schedule and realize I have too many "to do's" on my list. Then I feel the Holy Spirit prompting me, *Take a few of them off. Use your wheels, Marilyn.*

About more serious issues, I have at times neglected to talk to God about major concerns like financial decisions, health needs, and what I should be doing and how and when I should be doing it. Without thinking deeply about it, I guess I've assumed those are issues I can take care of myself. I know better, but sometimes I have to fall flat and then remember. Romans 8:26 states:

"And the Holy Spirit helps us in our distress. For we don't even know what we should pray for, nor how we should pray. But the Holy Spirit prays for us with groanings that cannot be expressed in words."

You, as a new believer, and I, as an old believer, have a wonderful freedom to access the power of the very Spirit who lives within us. When we encounter problems involving marriage, kids, our finances, relatives—anything—the Holy Spirit "helps us in our distress." We are not alone. He knows, He cares, and He is there.

Some of you who are reading this booklet wish your problems were as simple as impatience, health, or decision making. Some of you are anguishing over issues of alcoholism, drug addiction, pornography, or promiscuity. How can the inner presence of the Holy Spirit help you deal with those huge challenges? Let me point you to a fantastically encouraging statement Jesus made; it's recorded in John 16:33:

"Here on earth you will have many trials and sorrows. But take heart, because I have overcome the world."

What did He mean? The world is full of many evils. Among them are the various addictions and unhealthy habits that shackle the human spirit. But Jesus said He had overcome all the evil in the world. Jesus is an overcomer. And He lives within you. So you, too, are an overcomer.

Remember Samson, the Old Testament character I referred to in chapter 3? When he and his parents were walking to a neighboring village, Samson was suddenly attacked by a young lion. He had an immediate need of "overcoming power," and he got it. "At that moment the Spirit of the LORD powerfully took control of him, and he ripped the lion's jaws apart with his bare hands" (Judges 14:6).

There are some addictions and other unhealthy habits that can be as life threatening as an unexpected lion attack. When they hit, you feel so weak your legs collapse. Samson was not personally equipped to rip the lion's jaws apart. But the Holy Spirit was—and is. You are not personally equipped to rip apart the jaws of whatever has power over you. You need strength other than your own. You need the strength of the Holy Spirit. Don't forget that it's there, waiting for you to tap into it. Psalm 138:3 says:

"When I pray, you answer me; you encourage me by giving me the strength I need." Honey, you've got wheels. Don't forget to use them!

Assurance Questions

1. Describe a time when you needed power but thought you had to provide that power yourself.

2. What would you do differently now?

3. What do you think about the expression "God helps those who help themselves"? Do you think we ought to do as much for ourselves as possible before calling on the Holy Spirit?

4. Is it healthy to be totally dependent on Spirit power? Why or why not?

5. Are there some areas of your life you'd like to leave the Holy Spirit out of? Why?

GOD BENDS DOWN TO LISTEN

Prayer is the key to accessing the power of the Holy Spirit within you. You open your mouth and use your words. You open your heart and reveal your concern. You unite with the Spirit in the knowledge He will answer you. In its most simplified form, that is prayer. Prayer is talking to God.

My daughter, Beth, is teaching her six-year-old son, Alec, to pray out loud. He has been reluctant to hear his own little voice addressing God. He's afraid his words "won't sound right." So Beth is coaching him on his words. When they come together to pray, Beth tells Alec she will say a phrase and then Alec can repeat the phrase. Beth will say another phrase, and Alec will repeat it. Yesterday, before the evening meal, Alec was going to pray, again with his mother's coaching. The prayer began with, "Thank You, God, for this great day. Thank You for this food. And could You help me understand numbers?"

Alec's head shot up as Beth asked God for numerical assistance, and he said, "Can I say *that* to God?" He was astounded that prayer was not just thanking God for food and safety. It's also about the stuff in our lives and the needs of our souls. Understanding numbers is a basic need in Alec's life right now.

The moment we begin talking to God and making our needs known, we are accessing the power of the Spirit. As the psalmist wrote, "When I pray, you answer me." God hears us and begins immediately to help us with the concerns in our lives. First John 5:14–15 says:

"We can be confident that he will listen to us whenever we ask him for anything in line with his will. And if we know he is listening when we make our requests, we can be sure that he will give us what we ask for."

That's why we talk to God about everything. He listens, He cares, and He works for us. That praying accesses the Spirit power within us.

Now, let's pause just a moment to key into a phrase in the 1 John verse. Notice that it says, "Whenever we ask him for anything in line with his will." That phrase is a safety net for us. We may not always pray for what is within the will of God. For example, it is never in the will of God that we pray for something contrary to what is morally right. God has provided right-living standards for us, and it is never His will that we break those standards.

For example, remember Holly in chapter 2? She prayed that the man with whom she was having an affair would divorce his wife and marry Holly. Her rationalization was that it would be good for their yet-to-be-born child. But that request was not in line with God's will. Now, that does not mean the man might not divorce his wife and marry Holly. He could choose to do so, but it would not be because God willed it or the Holy Spirit empowered it.

I love the way *The Message* translation of the Bible presents 1 Peter 1:17. It states:

"You call out to God for help and he helps—he's a good Father that way. But don't forget, he's also a responsible Father, and won't let you get by with sloppy living."

There's great security in realizing we can pray for the desires of our heart while knowing God is not going to allow "sloppy living."

Does it appear that Holly got away with sloppy living? Remember, she was a believer and a receiver of Christ. So where was the Holy Spirit in her life? Why didn't He protect her from her own unwise desires and subsequent choices? The sobering truth is that we can choose to ignore the Spirit of God living within us. We can choose to ignore what we know to be God's moral law, which was designed to protect us from ourselves. We can refuse His overcoming power. He does not force us to abandon our unwise choices or to live in His power.

By the same token, there is no peace or joy in the life of a sinning Christian. When a Christian determines to continue living in sin, it's like walking with sharp little rocks in your shoes. Each step is uncomfortable. That's one of the ways God does not let us get by with sloppy living. It is miserable. But if we want the rocky walk, if we are willing to pay the price, we can have it. There's no knock-you-down, drag-you-around style with God. We can choose.

But here's an interesting postscript to the Holly story. She ultimately came to the realization that her choices only produced difficult consequences, and she longed to be reinstated in a relationship with God. She missed Him. She was tired of walking on sharp rocks. She was tired of feeling soiled. She longed to be forgiven.

But she wasn't sure how to "get back with" God. What could she say? And how could she say it? Had He run out of patience with her? How could she convince Him she was sincere this time?

Holly had gotten some therapy and had learned that she had a strong need for male affirmation. That need had led her down a sloppy path. How would she talk to God about her need for male affirmation?

Would He think it was just psycho-babble? What did He think of therapy anyway? Surely that's not what you talk to God about.

What Holly ultimately learned is the same thing Beth taught little Alec: You talk to God about everything. She remembered the assurance from 1 John 5:14: "We can be confident that he will listen to us."

So Holly started talking (praying) to God. She told Him she was ashamed of her behavior. She told Him she wanted to be a good mom. She told Him she needed help to stop flirting with men. In other words, she told God everything. She quit worrying about her words and how they sounded. She prayed out of her heart. With those prayers came assurance of forgiveness and, to her amazement, an inner power and strength she had never experienced before. If a young lion walked through her neighborhood representing a compelling new male possibility, she felt sure she could, empowered by the Holy Spirit, rip open the jaws of that lion and then walk away.

We have the assurance of the Holy Spirit living

within us. We have the assurance that prayer ignites His power to meet our needs. And we have the assurance that even when our prayer requests may be out of line, He will not let us get by with "sloppy living."

Prayer is talking to God. With confidence, we echo the wishes of David stated in Psalm 5:3:

"Listen to my voice in the morning, LORD. Each morning I bring my requests to you and wait expectantly." It's a much better way to start your day than filling your shoes with gravel!

ASSURANCE QUESTIONS

1. Do you pray much? How do you pray? How do you feel when you pray? Do you worry God may not hear you?

2. Psalm 116:1–2 says, "I love the LORD because he hears and answers my prayers. Because he bends down and listens, I will pray as long as I have breath!" Can you visualize God bending down to hear your prayers?

3. Write God a prayer that reflects exactly how you feel right now. Read it aloud to Him. As you are reading it, picture God bending down and listening to you.

4. Does seeing that image of God make prayer seem more personal and meaningful to you? If so, can you describe how or why?

A Book More Appealing Than Chocolate Chip Ice Cream

When Jeff was five years old, I snuggled up with him one evening shortly before his bedtime and suggested we read a Bible story together. Always sensitive about hurting others' feelings, Jeff hesitated and then asked, "Is there anything else we could do?"

"Well, what do you have in mind?" I asked.

"How about chocolate chip ice cream? We could each have a bowl," he answered. So we both had a bowl of chocolate chip ice cream and *then* read a Bible story together.

As a new believer in Christ, you may feel an interest in the Bible you did not formerly have. It may now be more appealing than even a bowl of chocolate chip ice cream. That new interest in the Bible is yet another evidence of the Holy Spirit living within you. You probably have an appetite to know as much as you can about your new faith. Matthew 5:6 states, "Blessed are those who hunger and thirst for righteousness, for they shall be filled" (NKJV). One of the ways we are "filled" and satisfied is by studying the Bible.

So how does one start studying the Bible? First, you want to be aware that the Bible is not just a moral guidebook or a list of directions for better living. Though you will be inspired by its moral teachings and will certainly learn principles meant to save you from the consequences of poor decisions, the Bible is more than that. It is a divinely inspired Book meant to communicate a personal message: God knew you and loved you before He even made you. That message is expressed throughout the Bible in passages like this one:

"Long before he laid down earth's foundations, he had us in mind, had settled on us as the focus of his love" (Ephesians 1:4 MSG).

You will find this theme throughout the Bible. The Bible is God's voice speaking that message of passionate love to each of us. He is exceedingly passionate about His creation!

So where do you begin? Because the Bible is literally a library of books, you can begin reading anywhere. Should you start at the very beginning and begin reading Genesis? You certainly can. But I would suggest you begin reading the first four books in the New Testament because there you get a great picture of who Jesus is, what He said, what He did, and why He did it. Those books—Matthew, Mark, Luke, and John—are similar because all four are accounts of Jesus's life. They are wonderfully instructive; as you read them, you will become increasingly familiar with Jesus. You will hear from Him the theme again and again that we, God's creation, were, are, and will always be the "focus of his love."

Linger as long as you want in those books. By studying them, you are receiving foundational truth as you assimilate what you learn about Jesus, something that is very satisfying for you who "hunger and thirst." When you feel like it, I'd suggest you then begin reading the book of Acts, which follows Mark.

Acts details what happened after Jesus left the earth. The disciples were told to get out there and spread the good news of Jesus. The book chronicles the beginning of the first Christian church and many of the harrowing experiences that contributed to its growth. Jesus told the disciples their jobs would not be greater than their abilities because the Holy Spirit would enable them when they felt weak and afraid. You will remember one of the great sports for the Romans in those days was feeding Christians to the lions. You can imagine the need, then, for the empowering of the Holy Spirit for those early Christians! Many died for their faith. (In these cases the Spirit did not empower them to rip open the jaws of the attacking lions.)

We also see in the book of Acts how Christianity rose out of Judaism. The early Christians acknowledged Jesus as the Messiah, but these new Christians

remained deeply committed to their Jewish tradi-
tions. They struggled when the Holy Spirit nudged
them to take the message of Jesus's love to the
Gentiles. It did not make sense to them that God
could possibly love the Gentiles and that Jesus's
death on the cross offered forgiveness for Gentiles'
sin as well as their own.

Also in Acts you will read about Paul, a highly
educated and articulate Jewish scholar who despised
all he heard about the impostor-Messiah named
Jesus. Paul, with his intellect and political power,
was determined to see that all Christians were tor-
tured, imprisoned, or murdered for their offensive
faith in Jesus.

However, God had Paul in mind long before the
foundations of the earth were laid. Paul was the
"focus" of God's love. You'll be fascinated with
the account of Paul's trip to Damascus. I'm sure
you can guess what happened.

If I found myself exiled to the little town of
Abscessed Molar, Texas (ten miles south of Puffy
Gums), and was given a choice of what Bible book

I could take with me, it would be the book of Romans. It follows the book of Acts.

After Paul's dramatic conversion, he responded to the passionate love of God by teaching, preaching, and writing about the Jesus he came to know personally and love intensely. The book of Romans is a long letter Paul wrote to a group of first-century Christians in Rome. In it he brilliantly and passionately described how it is possible that sinful human beings can find acceptance with God. It is in Romans that we read, "There is no condemnation for those who belong to Christ Jesus" (8:1). We are not only accepted by God, but our sin no longer condemns us. We are free from the sin shackles that enslaved us and kept us in bondage. What is the source of that freedom? Jesus! His death on the cross for all sin puts us in the elite category of those without condemnation.

Romans 5:1–2 says, "Since we have been made right in God's sight by faith, we have peace with God because of what Jesus Christ our Lord has done for us. Because of our faith, Christ has brought us into this place of highest privilege where we now stand, and we confidently and joyfully look forward to sharing God's glory."

What peace and sweet assurance those words produce! Such words, inspired by the Holy Spirit of God within the born-again spirit of Paul, cause us to again see the depth of God's focused love for us. Romans is a book you will want to read over and over again. I wouldn't go into exile without it. In fact, I don't want to go anywhere without it.

Now, you may be wondering about the Old Testament and when you should start reading it. You can, of course, start anytime. My suggestion, however, is that after you've absorbed the life and words of Jesus, and after you read Acts and Romans, you then begin reading the Old Testament.

I recommend that you begin by reading the people stories. There are many people stories in Genesis, and there are also full books of people stories: Joshua, Ruth, Ezra, Job, Jonah, and Hosea, for example. I'd suggest you read the entire story of each person rather than stop at the end of a chapter within the book. (Someone else can cook dinner!) I love reading these stories because I see myself in so many of them. Though centuries, customs, and languages separate us, we are united by the same heart cries. And in all that we read, we are the focused love of God.

The book of Psalms is a compilation of prayers that were meant to be prayed aloud. They are a tremendous comfort to those of you who feel you're not ready yet to open your mouth in prayer. You may feel your words won't sound good enough. You'll see that there is nothing polished or refined about the language in the Psalms prayers. They are sometimes whiny, happy, confused, faltering, repetitious, and uncertain. In other words, the Psalms use real words to express real emotion. You can literally pray the Psalms to God. Choose one, then read it aloud to God as your expression to Him. In time, doing so will not feel awkward. You will find your own spirit uniting with the spirit of the words as if you had written them yourself.

I suggest you save the prophetic books of Isaiah, Jeremiah, and Ezekiel until a later study. The same is true for the books of God's law: Leviticus, Numbers, and Deuteronomy. You will ultimately benefit from reading them, but it's OK to wait awhile before you dive into them.

And by the way, it's always beneficial to have a standard study Bible to help you in your understanding of Scripture. Study Bibles have notes and cross references that help you understand each passage and put it into perspective.

It may be confusing to you to notice there are a number of translations of the Bible. You may wonder, *What does that mean? Why aren't they the same? Is one better than another? Which one should I read?*

It helps to understand that the Hebrew and Greek Bible has come down to us through the meticulous scholarship of ancient scribes who copied the original text in successive generations. There are two points of view about how that scholarship should be presented to us as modern-day readers. The first is that the translation may be a thought-for-thought, or paraphrase, translation. According to that view, modern-day readers do not miss the original meaning of the passages, but the language is recognizable, everyday usage.

For example, a popular translation that uses everyday language and paraphrases but is careful to preserve the original scriptural meaning is *The Message*. Consider the wording of Psalm 56:1–4 from *The Message*:

Take my side, God—I'm getting kicked around,
    stomped on every day.
Not a day goes by
    but somebody beats me up;
They make it their duty
    to beat me up.

When I get really afraid
    I come to you in trust.
I'm proud to praise God;
    fearless now, I trust in God.
    What can mere mortals do?

It may give some of you whiplash to read the sentence, "Take my side, God—I'm getting kicked around." Perhaps you're tempted to purse your lips and say, "Is that any way to talk to God?" The rationale for *The Message* translation is, this is how the writer of the psalm was feeling. He told it as it was! For many readers, that emotional candor with God is a comfort. We can truly talk to Him without worrying about how our words sound.

The other point of view does not criticize verbal openness with God but is concerned with a literal and precise effort to translate Scripture word for word. This kind of translation is not a paraphrase of thoughts; it is a word-by-word rendering of the original Greek and Hebrew texts. An excellent translation committed to this point of view is the New King James Bible. Consider the same passage, Psalm 56:1–4, that you read above from *The Message* now in the New King James version. The meaning in both is clear. The language differs.

Be merciful to me, O God, for man would
    swallow me up;
Fighting all day he oppresses me.
My enemies would hound me all day,
For there are many who fight against me, O
    Most High.

Whenever I am afraid,
I will trust in You.
In God (I will praise His word),
In God I have put my trust;
I will not fear.
What can flesh do to me?

As you begin your study of Scripture, choose
those translations with which you feel comfortable.
You may want to have several translations. I have
almost all of them. My favorite for teaching and
writing is the New Living Translation. Unless passages are otherwise identified, that's the version
quoted throughout this booklet. But my favorite
for personal study is the New King James. The

important point is that we study God's words to us. By them we are fed.

Finally, I strongly urge you to get involved in a group Bible study. I'm a firm believer in the value each of us brings to the other. As you study together, share together, and pray together, a rich bond is established. That bond deepens as you feel loved and accepted by each other. Together you grow in your understanding of what it means to be a Christian and what it means to be the passionate focus of God's love.

Also, I'm sure that environment could be greatly enriched by the occasional sharing of chocolate chip ice cream.

ASSURANCE QUESTIONS

1. Have you read the Bible before? Were you bored, interested, confused, or turned off? How do you feel now about starting to read and study the Bible? Where do you plan to begin?

2. Second Timothy 3:16 says, "All Scripture is inspired by God." What does that mean? What does that say about the various authors of the books in the Bible?

3. Do you have a preference yet about a Bible translation? Which is it and why?

4. How do you feel about a group Bible study? Does a group have advantages over doing your private study? Could you not do both?

5. What's the most interesting fact you know about the Bible?

WHAT THE GLOW
OF GRACE LOOKS LIKE

At 6:45 p.m. on Sunday, May 4, 2003, a tornado ripped through Pierce City, Missouri, taking one life and eighty-one homes as well as the city hall and all but three of the town's forty-five businesses. It took about ten seconds. One eyewitness said he had a feeling he wasn't in Missouri anymore; it looked more like the photos he'd seen of Baghdad. Brick buildings that had been there since the 1880s suddenly crumbled.

The owner of the town's supermarket was in a hospital in nearby Springfield when the tornado took out the store he and his wife had owned for sixteen years. When he returned to the scene of devastation, he described what happened next:

"They came in with a loader, scooped up the rubble of my store, and put it in a Dumpster."

Here's where the story ceases to be just a news item. As the town settled down and began moving toward reconstruction, the grocery-store owner inquired if he could buy the property owned by the Baptist church. The church had put the property up for sale prior to the tornado, planning to build a new facility outside of town. The pastor and his board discussed the selling of their property to the grocer but decided against it. Instead the church simply gave it to him. Their explanation: "The town needs a grocery store, and we were going to move anyway."

The town pharmacist also needed to rebuild and asked the grocery-store owner if he would sell him the old grocery-store property. (Why they were playing musical properties, I don't know.) The grocer said he wouldn't sell it, but he'd give it to the pharmacist. The logic: It just seemed the right thing to do.

Since the city hall was destroyed and the town

required a bigger plot of land for rebuilding, the mayor asked the pharmacist if the city could buy his old property. You guessed it. The pharmacist responded, "I'm not going to take anything for it. You can have it."

It's unusual to see people extending such generosity and kindness to one another. It isn't unheard-of, but it does go contrary to the opportunistic inclinations of many persons. All too often we hear stories of the robbing and looting of innocent people at a time of environmental crisis.

Instead the people in Pierce City, Missouri, showed what grace looks like. The dictionary definition of *grace* is "a favor rendered by one who need not do so." The people of Pierce City did not need to come to each other's aid. No one forced them to do so; they simply chose to. In so doing, the little town basks in the glow of grace.

As Christians we also bask in the glow of grace, but ours is the grace of God. The grace of God differs from the grace of people simply because people *sometimes* come through, as they did in

Missouri, and sometimes they don't. The giving of human grace may depend on temperament, circumstances, or level of personal generosity. God, however, is constant and totally committed to giving grace to His people. His grace is not dependent upon His temperament, circumstances, or level of personal generosity. The bestowing of grace is a part of God's divine intent and passionate love. Next to your salvation experience, grace is the most important facet of God's love.

Jesus told a story about a prodigal son that was designed to show us what God's grace looks like. In abbreviated form, here's the story Jesus told. (You can read it for yourself in Luke 15.)

The prodigal was a kid who was full of himself, bored with his circumstances, and dying to get away from home. He had the colossal nerve to ask his father for his portion of the inheritance money that would come to him after the father's death. Amazingly, the father gave it to him. The son ran off to the "far country" and ultimately squandered every last penny of that inheritance.

Hungry and desperate, he got a job feeding pigs. He soon found himself craving the very slop he fed the hogs. Mired in the muck of the pigsty, the boy realized how stupid he had been, how even his father's servants ate better than he was eating. Feeling appropriately ashamed of himself, he turned in the direction of home with the intent of begging his father's forgiveness. We'll finish the story as it is told in *The Message*.

When he was still a long way off, his father saw him. His heart pounding, he ran out, embraced him, and kissed him. The son started his speech: "Father, I've sinned against God, I've sinned before you; I don't deserve to be called your son ever again."

But the father wasn't listening. He was calling to the servants, "Quick. Bring a clean set of clothes and dress him. Put the family ring on his finger and sandals on his feet. Then get a grain-fed heifer and roast it. We're going to feast! We're going to have a wonderful time!

My son is here—given up for dead and now alive! Given up for lost and now found!"

According to Eastern custom, the son did not deserve such an enthusiastic, loving, and forgiving reception. His father had every reason to forbid his son to ever come onto the family property again. The boy had dishonored his father and brought shame upon the family name. According to their customs, the boy deserved to be disowned.

But Jesus told the story to illustrate how our heavenly Father extends grace to us beyond human understanding and custom. He told the story to illustrate that not one of us is ever disowned by the Father in spite of our behavior. Just as the prodigal's father daily scanned the horizon in the hope of his son's return, so too does our Father. God waits for us. When it dawns on us we're mired in a pigsty and we rush home in repentance and regret, the Father receives us with open arms. That's what divine grace looks like.

Perhaps you're familiar with the old hymn

"Amazing Grace." Of all the songs ever written, this one has been recorded the greatest number of times by the greatest number of vocal artists. It was written by John Newton, a slave trader turned preacher.

> Amazing grace! How sweet the sound
> That saved a wretch like me!
> I once was lost but now am found.
> Was blind, but now I see.

Were it not for the centuries that separated Newton and the young prodigal, I'm sure the lad would have hummed that hymn repeatedly as he found himself reinstated and safe in his father's forgiveness and embrace.

You may be wondering if there is a distinction to be made between God's love and God's grace. Doesn't all forgiveness spring from God's love? Yes, it does. Were it not for God's love, there would be no grace. But I want to put an emphasis on the grace facet of God's love because it enables us to see more clearly the whole picture of God's love.

For example, the prodigal did not deserve forgiveness. He did nothing even to try to earn it. In fact, he did everything he could to make himself unworthy of forgiveness. God's love (grace) declares us worthy even though we are not. Human grace may not find us worthy or able to see past our unattractive behavior. But God's grace never wavers.

We are worthy because Jesus made us worthy by paying the penalty for our sin. Romans 6:23 says, "The wages of sin is death." That is God's standard. But Jesus fulfilled the law. We did not die; He died instead. His death satisfied the law of God that sin be punished by death. Therefore we can be forgiven and made secure in a divine acceptance we did not earn and were not worthy of in the first place.

Many Christians feel they need to do things for God as a way of earning His grace and love. Those people believe they need to be better and better Christians so God will be glad His Son died for them. But that is not how grace/love operates. *It's a gift.* Not a solitary thing you do (none of your "works") will make you good enough for His grace. Jesus already made you good enough.

In the straightforward language of *The Message*, we read:

"Now God has us where he wants us, with all the time in this world and the next to shower grace and kindness upon us in Christ Jesus. Saving is all his idea, and all his work. All we do is trust him enough to let him do it. It's God's gift from start to finish! We don't play the major role. If we did, we'd probably go around bragging that we'd done the whole thing!" (Ephesians 2:7–9).

If we don't "play the major role," what do we play? Surely there are rules we need to follow in an effort to cooperate with the "grace and kindness" God has shown to us. How do we do the Christian life if God says we are to "trust him enough to let him do it"? Do we just grab a box of Milk Duds and head for the hammock?

In the next chapter, we'll talk about the meaning of that phrase "trust him enough to let him do it" and how liberating that truth is in the way we live our Christian lives. If you wish, you can munch and sway while you read about it.

ASSURANCE QUESTIONS

1. What's the difference between God's grace and God's love? Does knowing that distinction make a difference in how you view God?

2. When have you experienced "people grace"? When have you *extended* people grace?

3. Would you have forgiven the prodigal son? Why or why not?

4. How hard or easy is it for you to receive a "favor rendered by one who need not do so"? Do you try to return the favor? Do people expect you to? Does God?

5. How do you interpret the Ephesians 2 statement that if we had anything to do with bringing about our salvation "we'd go around bragging that we'd done the whole thing"? Does that fit your thinking? Does it offend you?

8

FROM DEATH TO LIFE

John 11 provides a graphic and memorable account of a dead man. His name was Lazarus. He and his sisters were close friends with Jesus. Their home frequently provided a place for food and rest for Jesus as He traveled in the area. When Lazarus got sick, the sisters frantically called for Jesus to come, but He arrived too late. By the time He arrived, Lazarus had been dead for four days.

At Jesus's request, Martha, one of the sisters, led Jesus to the grave. It was a cave with a large boulder sealing its entrance. When Jesus commanded that the stone be rolled away, Martha protested and said, "Lord, by now the smell will be terrible because he has been dead for four days" (John 11:39). But in obedience to Jesus, she had the stone rolled away. And guess what happened next.

"Then Jesus shouted, 'Lazarus, come out!' And Lazarus came out, bound in graveclothes, his face wrapped in a headcloth. Jesus told them, 'Unwrap him and let him go!'" (John 11:43–44).

What in the world is that story about? And what does it have to say to us? Scripture says we are all dead because of our sin. Ephesians 2:1 states, "Once you were dead, doomed forever because of your many sins." And 1 Peter 4:6 says, "The gospel was preached also to those who are dead" (NKJV). Scripture describes those who have not received Christ as dead people . . . dead in their sin . . . dead because they have no spiritual life. At one time we were all a Lazarus, bound up in graveclothes, dead and stinking in our sins. But then Jesus called us to life. We have been called from the grave of sin to a new state of spiritual life.

Did Lazarus have the will, the determination, the ability to roll that stone away, throw off the binding graveclothes, and walk out into the sunlight? Of course not. How did he do it? He was called by Jesus.

He was called from death to life. You and I also have been called from death to life. Our will or determination or personal abilities has nothing to do with that calling. As *The Message* puts it, "It's God's gift from start to finish!" (Ephesians 2:8).

It is also God's gift that enables us to live our Christian life without tripping over our own graveclothes. Jesus said to unwrap Lazarus and let him go. He says the same thing to us.

How do we get bound up in graveclothes if we are no longer dead? It happens when we refuse to admit our powerlessness. It happens when we think our walk with God will be successful, based on our abilities instead of His.

God's people learned about their powerlessness when they received the Ten Commandments. At first they thought it felt good to know just exactly what it would take to make God happy. All they had to do was follow the rules, keep God's laws. Then they discovered they could keep some of the laws but not all of them. They could stop themselves from murdering but not from envying. They could stop themselves from adultery but not from lusting—and on and on.

God knew all along they couldn't keep the laws. He wasn't doing a 'nah-nah-ne-nah-nah' to His people when it dawned on them they were failing at rule keeping. God knew they'd fail at it. The point of the law was to show His people they needed a Savior. They could never make themselves good enough for God. He demands perfection. The Old Testament law was intended to demonstrate to the people their inability to be perfect.

Doesn't it seem odd then that the desire for rules persists in our thinking today? We understand we are no longer dead. We understand God demands perfection, which we couldn't achieve, so Jesus did it for us. We understand that the Holy Spirit lives within us and is our power source. But in spite of that knowledge, we reach for the grave-clothes and bind ourselves up with a list of rules. Maybe your list of rules would look like this:

1. Read your Bible every day (minimum thirty minutes).

2. Pray every day (minimum thirty minutes).

3. Join a church.

4. Be baptized.

5. Serve on church committees.

6. Stop drinking.

7. Stop smoking.

8. Stop swearing.

9. Give a portion of your income to your church and other Christian organizations.

10. Cut back on chocolate.

11. Memorize five verses (minimum) of Scripture each week.

12. Never criticize or gossip.

You may now have stopped the hammock, dropped the Milk Duds box, and started thinking, *That's a long list, but I think I could do it (except for the chocolate). All it would take is a disciplined regimen and determination.*

If you're thinking that way, you've already slipped into the trap of self-effort and self-motivation. That is not "trusting him enough to let him do it." You're attempting a program where the emphasis is trusting yourself, and that's a form of legalistic discipline. You're planning to follow the rules and counting on your personal discipline to carry it off.

Legalistic discipline is about obligation. It's about "doing it right." When our life is driven by obligation, we soon lose our desire to talk to God, to revel in what He did for us, and to assume a "trusting him enough to let him do it" attitude. Legalistic discipline causes us to be too busy with the timer during Bible study, prayer, and Scripture memorization to enjoy our new life as a Christian.

Also what is sobering about legalistic discipline is that it not only refits us for graveclothes, it sends us back into the tomb. We're not dead, but it feels like it. Fortunately, Jesus called us out of there, and He also said to get unwrapped.

The subtle lure of legalistic discipline is, it looks good. There's nothing wrong with the rules we listed. In fact, they are rules we may want to consider. No, the problem with rules is not the rules themselves but how we determine to keep them: through *obligation* to God or through *love* of God. If it's obligation, sooner or later we're going to tire of feeling obligated. Sooner or later our well-intentioned discipline will fail us. Why? Because in ourselves, we are weak.

That brings us to the subject of my thumbs. (Of course it does, Marilyn! You're *so* easy to follow.)

Over the last few months, I've developed increasing discomfort and a new weakness in my thumbs. When I need to take the lid off a water bottle, for example, I wander helplessly about in search of an able-bodied thumb person. What's that about? I'm told it's arthritis.

Understanding my new weakness, would I benefit from the discipline of at least thirty minutes of thumb exercises a day? Would I find a measure of relief by increasing my determination to twist off the tops of water bottles without a grimace? How many times a day should I repeat my efforts at the non-grimace cap-twist? Just what is my obligation to my thumbs? Mercy!

The opposite approach to living out our new Christian life is based on love for God and not obligation to Him. Jesus said in John 14:15, "If you love me, obey my commandments." He did not say, "If you don't keep my commandments, your children will have crooked teeth for the next four generations." He didn't say, "You better do what you're told, don't ask questions, and keep those commandments perfectly." There is no threat in Jesus's statement. There is an assumption that love produces a desire to obey.

You see, our love for God, our appreciation that He called us out of deadness, inspires a genuine eagerness to read the Bible, talk to Him in prayer, and memorize verses that are personal, portable power packs for our "dailiness." Because I love Him, I *want* to attend church, share my earnings with Him, and address those behaviors that have produced ungodly habits. That desire springs from love, not obligation.

That love of God is the key to trusting Him enough to let Him "do it." Do what? Everything! Absolutely everything. The joy of responding to God's love for us comes in the partnership He offers us in overcoming our difficulties. We are not alone in them. He partners with us by providing the wisdom and strength—and even abstinence from those life issues that threaten to derail us. In our love for Him, in our trust of Him, we receive from Him all we are not. This is what it means to "let him do it." He invites us to climb off the tread-mill of self-effort and rule keeping.

I'm in periodic correspondence with a woman who struggles with alcoholism. She is a pastor's wife in a relatively small community. One of her greatest fears is being "found out." She knows all the scriptures, and she knows God has not dis-owned her. But the grip of alcohol continues its hold upon her.

How would this woman let God "do it" for her? Would she just head for the hammock and substi-tute Milk Duds for a bottle?

Letting God "do it" is not a passive action. We partner with Him. He has the power; we do not. We recognize His power, and in our powerlessness we pray, "Jesus, help me!"

That He *will* help us is a given.

What is the pastor's wife's responsibility in letting God "do it"? She needs to choose to trust Him. She also needs to admit her powerlessness. Oddly enough, she thinks it's only a matter of time before she's able to "conquer" her vice. She's working on increasing her discipline. She's also tripping over her graveclothes.

He didn't call her to rule keeping, even about something as destructive as alcoholism. He called her from death to life. He called her to a partnership of trust. In that partnership she can experience the power to overcome. Philippians 4:13 states, "I can do everything with the help of Christ who gives me the strength I need."

So can you. So can I. That's the role we play. It's not the major role. God plays the major role while we rest in who He is and what He has done and in the knowledge that we were, are, and will always be the focus of His love. And that powerful love is what brings us from death to life.

ASSURANCE QUESTIONS

1. Do you see yourself as a Lazarus? How?

2. Do you trip over your graveclothes? If so, do you know how and why?

3. Read the whole story of Lazarus in John 11. Why did Jesus wait to come to Mary and Martha? How do you feel about His reasons?

4. Do you have any rules you think you need to follow? What are they? Why are they important to you? Are they necessary?

5. What is a legalist? Is there a problem with legalism? Where would you feel most comfortable: with a set of rules that made it clear what you should or should not do—or trusting your love of God to direct your behavior?

CONCLUSION:
CHRIST *LIVES* IN YOU!

There's a knock on Saint Peter's door. He looks out and a man is standing there. Saint Peter is about to begin his interview when the man disappears. A short time later there's another knock. Saint Peter gets the door, sees the man, opens his mouth to speak—and the man disappears again.

"Hey!" Saint Peter calls after him. "Are you playing games with me?"

"No," the man's distant voice replies anxiously, "I'm in a hospital, and they keep trying to resuscitate me!"

This poor guy didn't know if he was coming or going. I am hoping that after you've read and studied this booklet you will have no uncertainty about the direction your life is taking. I hope you'll feel absolute assurance of God's love for you, His total forgiveness of all your sin, and your worthiness to be a member of His family. It's a done deal! There's no waffling on God's part. You belong to Him, and He won't let you go.

You will have times, as we all do, when you will feel overwhelmed by your circumstances and even scared for your future. When that happens, don't come and go in your faith in the Father. Instead, listen and be encouraged by these words from Philippians 4:

"Don't fret or worry. Instead of worrying, pray. Let petitions and praises shape your worries into prayers, letting God know your concerns. Before you know it, a sense of God's wholeness, everything coming together for good, will come and settle you down. It's wonderful what happens when Christ displaces worry at the center of your life" (verses 6–7 MSG).

Christ not only "displaces worry at the center of your life," He *lives* in the center of your life! You can't find greater assurance than that!

A Word from

WOMEN OF FAITH®

The moment you make this decision to begin a personal relationship with God, through His Son, Jesus Christ, He comes into your life and, as He says in Hebrews 13: 5, "I will never leave you or forsake you." As Marilyn has explained, you can be absolutely assured of this regardless of your feelings at any given time. The Bible confirms our relationship with God, and we can be secure in that fact.

Becoming a believer in the Person of Christ can happen at a moment in time, but growing in your relationship with Him is the adventure of a lifetime. It's a process. We trust this booklet has helped you understand the great treasure you have in knowing Christ. And we hope it helped you begin to grasp all God has for you, his beloved child. Our prayer for you is that every day your relationship with Him will become more meaningful.